CAREERS FOR
HEROES

SMOKEJUMPERS

Emma Jones

PowerKiDS
press

New York

Published in 2016 by The Rosen Publishing Group, Inc.
29 East 21st Street, New York, NY 10010

First Edition

Editor: Katie Kawa
Book Design: Mickey Harmon

Photo Credits: Cover (woman) Fuse/Getty Images; cover (background) Sergii Votit/Shutterstock.com; cover, pp. 1, 3, 4, 6, 8, 10, 12, 14, 16–17, 18, 20, 22–24 (gray and yellow textures) siro46/Shutterstock.com; p. 4 Brad Wilson/Stone/Getty Images; p. 5 Idaho Statesman/Contributor/Tribune News Service/Getty Images; p. 7 https://en.wikipedia.org/wiki/555th_Parachute_Infantry_Battalion_(United_States)#/media/File:20111110-OC-AMW-0004_-_Flickr_-_USDAgov.jpg; p. 9 Holger Leue/Lonely Planet Images/Getty Images; p. 11 (inset) Nick Stubbs/Shutterstock.com; pp. 11 (main), 12, 18, 19 Justin Sullivan/Staff/Getty Images News/Getty Images; p. 13 David McNew/Staff/Getty Images News/Getty Images; p. 14 https://en.wikipedia.org/wiki/Fire_shelter#/media/File:Fire_shelter.jpg; p. 15 courtesy of Fort Wayne Public Affairs Office; pp. 21, 22 Tim Matsui/Stringer/Hulton Archive/Getty Images.

Cataloging-in-Publication Data

Jones, Emma.
Smokejumpers / by Emma Jones.
p. cm. — (Careers for heroes)
Includes index.
ISBN 978-1-5081-4391-8 (pbk.)
ISBN 978-1-5081-4392-5 (6-pack)
ISBN 978-1-4994-1853-8 (library binding)
1. Smokejumpers — Juvenile literature. 2. Wildfire fighters — Juvenile literature. I. Jones, Emma. II. Title.
SD421.23 J66 2016
634.9'618—d23

Manufactured in the United States of America

CPSIA Compliance Information: Batch #BW16PK: For Further Information contact Rosen Publishing, New York, New York at 1-800-237-9932

CONTENTS

INTO THE FIRE

When there's a fire in an area, most people are told to run away from it. However, the brave men and women who serve their communities as firefighters run toward fires. They work to put fires out and help people who can't get away from the flames.

Some firefighters actually jump from an airplane to fight fires! They're called smokejumpers, and they use **parachutes** to get from the sky to the ground. Their job is to help fight fires in areas that are hard to reach by traveling on the ground. They often parachute into the wilderness to fight wildfires.

FAST FACT!

About 400 smokejumpers are currently working in the United States. Both men and women can be smokejumpers.

Smokejumpers are brave people who fight fires in some of the most **remote** areas of the United States. Do you think you have what it takes to join their ranks? Read on to find out!

EARLY SMOKEJUMPERS

Smokejumpers have been parachuting to fires for over 75 years! The first smokejumping experiments took place in Washington State in 1939. The next year, the first successful jump to a fire was made in Idaho's Nez Perce National Forest.

One of the most famous teams of early smokejumpers was a group called the Triple Nickles. This group got its name from its military title, which was the 555th Airborne Battalion. The Triple Nickles were a group of African American men who became the first black **paratroopers** in U.S. history. During the summer of 1945, the Triple Nickles fought 36 fires throughout the American West.

FAST FACT!

Deanne Shulman was the first female smokejumper. She joined this special group of firefighters in 1981.

Members of the Triple Nickles, shown here, were heroic men who wanted to serve their country any way they could.

SMOKEJUMPER BASES

Who do smokejumpers work for? They're employed by the federal government, and they work for one of two government **agencies**: the Bureau of Land Management (BLM) and the U.S. Forest Service (USFS). Smokejumpers have nine main bases in the western United States.

Smokejumpers who work for the BLM work in Fairbanks, Alaska, or Boise, Idaho. The USFS also has bases in Idaho. These bases are located in McCall and Grangeville. Other USFS smokejumper bases include Redding, California, and Winthrop, Washington. An Oregon USFS base is located in Redmond, and USFS bases can also be found in West Yellowstone and Missoula in Montana.

FAST FACT!

The USFS employs more smokejumpers than the BLM. Over 270 of the smokejumpers currently working in the United States work for the USFS.

The largest smokejumper training base in the United States is located in Missoula, Montana. This base has a visitor center where you can learn more about smokejumping, and you can even take a tour of the base!

THE RIGHT PARACHUTE

It's easy to tell the difference between smokejumpers who work for the USFS and those who work for the BLM. All you need to do is look at their parachute. A smokejumper who works for the USFS uses a round parachute. A BLM smokejumper uses a square ram-air parachute. Ram-air parachutes are better parachutes in high winds, which BLM smokejumpers often face.

Smokejumpers fix their own parachutes. They also make their own jumpsuits, backpacks, and other gear. These men and women need to have good sewing skills, which they use when they're not fighting fires.

FAST FACT!

Smokejumpers spend the summer fighting fires. During the rest of the year, many of them work at sewing machines, making new gear and fixing torn parachutes.

The circular parachutes used by the USFS make it easier for smokejumpers to drop straight down. However, they don't work well when it's windy. That's why BLM smokejumpers use ram-air parachutes.

ON THE GROUND

After smokejumpers leave the airplane, they sometimes land in a tree. They train to get out of trees quickly and safely, and they also train to climb up and down trees to get a parachute that's stuck in the branches.

Smokejumpers then need to do what they jumped out of the plane to do—fight the fire! However, they don't use water. Instead, they use hand tools to dig a **trench** in front of the line of flames. They also cut down trees and other plants that could help the fire spread.

FAST FACT!

One of the only motorized tools smokejumpers use is a chainsaw. This helps them cut down trees that could serve as a path for the fire over their trench.

Smokejumpers such as this one sometimes start backfires. A backfire is a fire that's set to stop an advancing wildfire by clearing an area.

CLOTHING AND GEAR

When smokejumpers make their jumps, they don't look like the firefighters we often see in our communities. They wear a jumpsuit with padding that's meant to keep them safe during a hard landing. They also wear a helmet with a mask, which is supposed to **protect** them from tree branches. Heavy boots are also an important part of a smokejumper's gear.

Smokejumpers often carry a tent, as well as plenty of rope. A first aid kit is another important thing for a smokejumper to have, because it can take a long time for help to come if a smokejumper gets hurt.

FAST FACT!

Each smokejumper carries a fire shelter with them. A fire shelter is a kind of small tent with an outer **layer** made of foil. It's meant to protect a firefighter from heat for a short period of time.

Smokejumpers can carry as much as 115 pounds (52 kg) of gear with them as they walk through the burning wilderness.

BECOMING A SMOKEJUMPER

Because smokejumpers have to carry so much gear over rough land, they must be very fit. In fact, being able to pass a fitness test is an important requirement for becoming a smokejumper. Anyone who wants to become a smokejumper must be able to do a certain number of pull-ups, sit-ups, and push-ups, depending on which agency they want to work for. They also need to pass a running test.

Smokejumpers need to have firefighting **experience** or at least a four-year college degree. Many smokejumpers studied **forestry**, fire management, **engineering**, or science in college. Some smokejumpers work as teachers when they're not fighting fires.

FAST FACT!

During training, all smokejumpers must pass a test in which they carry 110 pounds (50 kg) of gear for 3 miles (4.8 km). They must do this in 90 minutes or less in order to pass.

Smokejumper Requirements

1 be at least 18 years old

2 be a U.S. citizen

3 have one year of related experience, a four-year college degree, or a combination of education and experience

4 have good hearing

5 have nearly perfect eyesight—glasses or contacts can be worn

6 be between 60 inches and 77 inches (152.4 and 195.6 cm) tall

7 weigh between 120 and 200 pounds (54.4 and 90.7 kg)

8 pass fitness tests

If you want to become a smokejumper, you'll need to make sure you meet these requirements.

LEARNING SMOKEJUMPING SKILLS

If you pass the tests to become a smokejumper, then your training starts. All smokejumpers go through training before the summer fire season begins. For rookie, or first-year, smokejumpers, this training involves using parachutes to make jumps, making a safe landing, and climbing trees.

Returning smokejumpers must pass a fitness test each year before they can get back to work. They're expected to stay in shape throughout their career. These smokejumpers also go through training to keep their skills sharp after months of not using them.

FAST FACT!

Rookie smokejumpers aren't expected to have parachuting skills before training starts. However, they're expected to have basic firefighting skills.

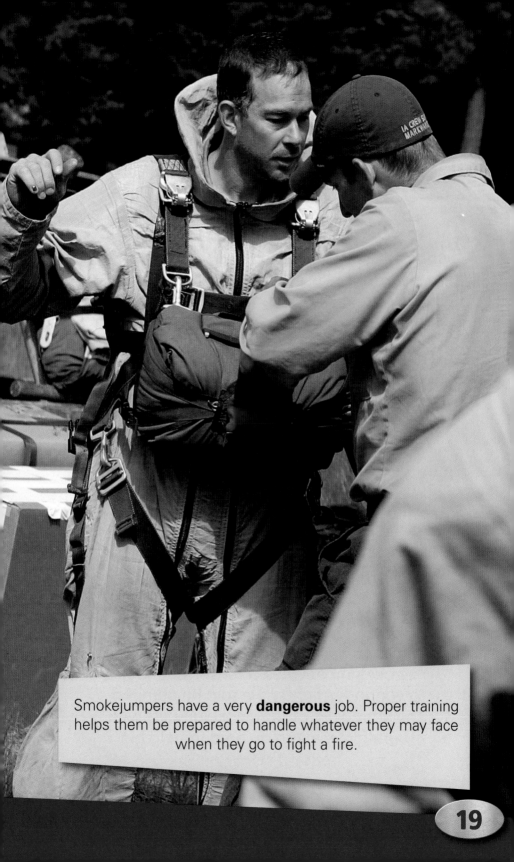

Smokejumpers have a very **dangerous** job. Proper training helps them be prepared to handle whatever they may face when they go to fight a fire.

A SMOKEJUMPER'S STORY

Jason Ramos is a smokejumper who knows how dangerous this job can be. He's also the co-author of a book about his life as a smokejumper, which is called *Smokejumper: A Memoir by One of America's Most Select Airborne Firefighters*.

Ramos has shared many stories from his smokejumping career with the public. These stories are filled with excitement and danger. Once, Ramos narrowly escaped a huge boulder that was rushing toward him as he fought a fire in Washington's North Cascade Mountains! Ramos is proud to be part of such a heroic group of men and women.

FAST FACT!

Ramos first knew he wanted to be a smokejumper when he was working as a young firefighter. He said he admired the hard work of the smokejumpers who would come into an area to help his fellow firefighters.

Jason
Ramos

Ramos worked as a smokejumper for over a decade before he shared his story with the world in 2015. Even after writing his book, he continued to work as a smokejumper.

AN UNCOMMON CAREER PATH

Becoming a smokejumper isn't a career path most people choose to follow. To become a smokejumper, you need to be brave, smart, and physically fit. You can prepare for a career as a smokejumper by working as hard as you can in science class. Smokejumpers need a good understanding of the science of fires and how fires affect living things.

If you think you have what it takes to be a smokejumper, visit a smokejumper base with an adult to learn more about this career. If you stay on this career path, you could become a hero who jumps to fires from the sky!

GLOSSARY

agency: A government department that is responsible for a certain activity or area.

dangerous: Not safe.

engineering: The study and practice of using math and science to do useful things, such as building machines.

experience: The length of time someone has been doing an activity.

forestry: The science and practice of caring for forests.

layer: One part of something lying over or under another part.

parachute: Something shaped like an umbrella and used when a person is falling through the air. Also, to jump from a high place and use a parachute to fall back to the ground.

paratrooper: A member of a group of soldiers who are trained to jump out of airplanes using a parachute.

protect: To keep safe.

remote: Far away.

trench: A long, narrow hole that is dug in the ground.

INDEX

WEBSITES

Due to the changing nature of Internet links, PowerKids Press has developed an online list of websites related to the subject of this book. This site is updated regularly. Please use this link to access the list: www.powerkidslinks.com/chero/smkj